SMILE-A-WHILE
TONGUE TWISTERS

By Gary Chmielewski
Drawings by Ron G. Clark

© 1986 Rourke Enterprises, Inc.

Library of Congress Cataloging in Publication Data

Chmielewski, Gary, 1946-
  Tongue twisters.

  (Smile-a-while joke book)
  Summary: A collection of sentences difficult to
say, for example: Which is the witch that wished the
wicked wish?
  1. Tongue twisters.   [1. Tongue twisters]
I. Title.   II. Series.
PN6371.5.C46   1986   818'.5402   86-17701
ISBN 0-86592-685-9

ROURKE ENTERPRISES, INC.
VERO BEACH, FLORIDA 32964

A skunk sat on a stump.
The stump thunk the skunk stunk.
The skunk thunk the stump stunk.

A bitter biting bittern bit a better brother bittern,
And the bitten better bittern bit the bittern biter back;
And the bitter bittern, bitten by the better bitten bittern,
Said, "I'm a bitter biting bittern bitten back!"

A pleasant place to place plates is a place where the plates are
pleased to be placed.

6.00

Silent snakes slipping slowly southwards.

Peter Piper picked a peck of pickled peppers.
Did Peter Piper pick a peck of pickled peppers?
If Peter Piper picked a peck of pickled peppers,
Where's the peck of pickled peppers Peter Piper picked?

These tricky tongue twisters give tender tongues blisters!

Especially suspicious spaghetti!

Gorgeous George ground Grim Greg greatly.

930320

Little Willie's wooden whistle wouldn't whistle.

Little Boy Blue blew a big blue bubble.

Do breath tests test the breath?
Yes, that's the best of a breath test.
So the best breath stands the breath test best!

Rubber baby-buggy bumpers.

Who washed Washington's white woolen underwear when Washington's washerwoman went West?

Double bubble gum bubbles double.

Thrice times three.
Twice times two.

Round and round the rugged rocks the ragged rascal ran.

Do drop in to the Dewdrop Inn.

Last year I could not hear with either ear.

If one doctor doctors another doctor, does the doctor who doctors the doctor doctor the doctor the way the doctor he is doctoring doctors? Or does he doctor the doctor the way the doctor who doctors doctors?

930320

I never smelled a smelt that smelled as bad as that smelt smelled.

Amidst the mist and coldest frosts,
With barest wrist and stoutest boasts,
He thrust his fist against the posts,
And still insists he sees the ghosts.

She sells seashells on the seashore.

Let us go together to gather lettuce, whether the weather
will let us or not.

"The bun is better buttered," Billy muttered.

The hunter killed him a great white bear.
With the skin he made him mittens.
Made them with the fur side inside.
Made them with the skin side outside.
So to get the cold side outside,
He put the warm side fur side inside;
And to get the warm side inside,
He put the inside skin side outside.

He ran from the Indies to the Andes in his undies!

Did you eever iver ever in you leaf life loaf
See the deevil divil devil kiss his weef wife woaf?
No, I neever niver never in my leaf life loaf
Saw the deevil divil devil kiss his weef wife woaf.

Cross crossings cautiously!

A library littered with literary literature.

Wood said he could carry the wood through the wood.
And if Wood said he could, Wood would carry the wood
through the wood.

Jim's twin sisters say tongue twisters.

Of all the ties I ever tied, I never tied a tie like this tie ties.

Did you ever see a gopher go for a gopher hole?
Yes! I saw a gopher go for a gopher hole when I was
going for the gopher.

I thought a thought, but the thought
I thought wasn't the thought
I thought I thought.
If the thought I thought I thought had been
the thought I thought, I wouldn't
have thought such a thought.

Sheep shouldn't sleep in a shack.
Sheep should sleep in a shed.

If a dog chews shoes, what shoes should he choose to chew?

We've tangled a twister or two.
Time for you to try turning a few!

Betty Botta bought some butter.
"But," said she, "this butter's bitter.
If I put it in my batter, it will make my batter bitter.
But a bit of better butter will but make my batter better."
So she bought a bit of butter better than the bitter butter.
It made her bitter batter better.

I can't stand rotten writing when it's written rotten.

She stops at the shops where I shop, and if she shops at the shop where I shop, I won't stop at the shop where she shops!

"Night, night, Knight," said one Knight to the other Knight the other night.

I saw Esau kissing Kate.
I saw Esau, he saw me.
And she saw that I saw Esau.

Of all the felt I ever felt
I never felt a piece of felt
That felt the same as the felt felt,
When I first felt that felt.

Pat's plump pop prunes plum trees promptly.

Good, better, best.
Never let it rest.
Till your good is better and your better best.

How much wood would a woodchuck chuck if a woodchuck could chuck wood?
A woodchuck would chuck as much wood as a woodchuck could chuck, if a woodchuck could chuck wood.

A maid with a duster made a furious bluster dusting a bust in the hall.
When the bust, it was dusted, the bust, it was busted.
The bust, it was dust, that is all!

A tutor who tooted a flute
Tried to tutor two tooters to toot.
Said the two to the tutor,
"Is it harder to toot, or
To tutor two tooters to toot?"

Peter Prangle, the prickly, prangly pear picker,
Picked three pecks of prickly, prangly pears
From the prangly pear trees on the pretty pleasant prairies.

He set to sea to see what he could see.

We eat what we can and what we can't we can.

Which is the witch that wishes the wicked wish?

Wriggly worms squirm regularly!

Zip! Zap! Zing! Zoom!   Bubbling blubber.

If a Hottentot taught a Hottentot tot to talk e'er the tot could totter,
Ought the Hottentot tot be taught to say aught, or naught, or what
ought to be taught her?
If to hoot and to toot a Hottentot tot be taught by a Hottentot tutor,
Should the tutor get hot if the Hottentot tot hoot and toot at the
Hottentot tutor?

> If a hair net could net hair,
> How much hair could that hair net net,
> If that hair net could net hair?

Of all the saws I ever saw saw,
I never saw a saw saw that could saw as this saw saws.

Poor Pop mopped slop when his pop bottle popped.

How many cans can a canner can if a canner can can cans?
A canner can can as many cans as a canner can if a canner can can cans

Nat said that that "that" was the right "that" in that place.

Will real wheels really wheel?

Beautiful babbling brooks bubble between blossoming banks.